Integrated Public Alert and Warning System (IPAWS)

Outreach Plan for Communications and Partner Engagement

FEMA   **May 2011**

IPAWS

Integrated Public Alert and Warning System

www.fema.gov/emergency/ipaws

This document replaces the
Integrated Public Alert and Warning System (IPAWS)
Stakeholder Engagement Plan dated March 2010

MESSAGE FROM THE DIRECTOR

May 2011

I am pleased to present this *Integrated Public Alert and Warning System (IPAWS) Outreach Plan for Communications and Partner Engagement*. This is the IPAWS Program Management Office (PMO) road map to engage Federal, State, local, tribal, and territorial government partners as well as our private sector partners in the public alert and warning domain.

Realizing the IPAWS Program will require the energy, effort and expertise of numerous individuals and organizations that have equities in public alert and warning, it is imperative that our public and private sector partners be informed, fully engaged, and committed to advancing alert and warning capabilities. IPAWS is not a capability that can be designed and mandated by the Federal Governement and then be expected to work properly in times of crisis. Rather, it is a collaborative effort to bring together the right resources – people, skills, and technologies to ensure the end result is an integrated and interoperable system allowing our Nation's leaders to alert and warn the American people.

Success in this endeavor depends on trusted relationships between and among government and private sector partners. The IPAWS Program Management Office is dedicated to ensuring these enduring relationships are fostered and maintainted to best serve the Nation. The American people are our most trusted partner in this critical program and during times of crisis have demonstrated resilience time and time again. Therefore, it is essential the American people have timely information to allow them to take the necessary actions to ensure their safety and minimize damage to property during times of crisis.

Antwane V. Johnson
Director
Integrated Public Alert and Warning System Program

TABLE OF CONTENTS

EXECUTIVE SUMMARY

The Integrated Public Alert and Warning System (IPAWS) program will modernize and enhance alert and warning delivery to the American public. Established by Presidential Executive Order 13407, the IPAWS Program brings together existing and new public alert and warning systems and technologies in order to provide government alerting authorities at all levels a broader range of message options and communications pathways.

During an emergency, the IPAWS will facilitate timely delivery of alert and warning information over more media to more people before, during, and after a disaster. In the event of a national emergency, the President will be able to use the IPAWS to send a message to the American people quickly and simultaneously through multiple communications pathways. The IPAWS will also provide Federal, State, local, tribal and territorial governments with capability to integrate their alert and warning systems with the national alert and warning infrastructure. Through this, the IPAWS will increase resilience of local systems and provide additional means by which life-saving information is distributed during a crisis.

The IPAWS Program Management Office (PMO) is partnering with recognized government and industry leaders and technical experts to ensure the IPAWS program incorporates the latest technologies and is practical for prospective users. Partners include Federal Governance and Legislative, Federal, State, local, tribal, and territorial Alerting Authorities, Private Sector Industry, Non-Profit and Advocacy, and the American People.

The effectiveness of the program will be realized through a comprehensive outreach approach using strategic communications and robust partnership engagement coupled with integrated training and exercises. The IPAWS PMO will also reach out to the American people to ensure they understand how the IPAWS functions, what it is for, what it provides, and how they can "Get Alerts, Stay Alive."

The Integrated Public Alert and Warning System (IPAWS) of the Federal Emergency Management Agency (FEMA), under Presidential Executive Order 13407, has clear directives to:

> ➢ Consult, coordinate, and cooperate with the private sector, including communications media organizations, and Federal, State, territorial, tribal and local governmental authorities, including emergency response providers;

> ➢ Ensure the conduct of public education efforts so that State, territorial, tribal, and local governments, the private sector, and the American people understand the functions of the public alert and warning system and how to access, use, and respond to information from the public alert and warning system; and,

> ➢ Ensure the conduct of training, tests, and exercises for the public alert and warning system.[1]

Additionally, in the 2009 General Accounting Office (GAO) report, *Improved Planning and Coordination Necessary for Modernization and Integration of Public Alert and Warning System*[2], the GAO recommended "increased coordination and consultation with partners."[3] The IPAWS Program Management Office (PMO) enthusiastically accepted the challenge evidenced by its *"Strategic Plan for the Integrated Public Alert and Warning System (IPAWS) Program – June 2010" ("Strategic Plan")*.

This IPAWS Outreach Plan establishes IPAWS' communication and partner engagement strategies to effectively accomplish the mission, vision, and goals stated in the IPAWS Strategic Plan. It also helps meet Executive Order 13407 directives and implements recommendations from the GAO report.

Outreach Goal 1: Provide partners with consistent messages at the right times

Objective 1.1: Create targeted messages for partners detailing IPAWS' purpose, scope, capabilities, benefits, limitations, and desired actions.

Objective 1.2: Disseminate timely information, materials, and updates to partners.

Objective 1.3: Provide feedback mechanisms to address partner concerns.

Outreach Goal 2: Engage and manage partners' expectations and activities effectively

Objective 2.1: Document and ensure understanding of partners' roles and responsibilities.

Objective 2.2: Secure partner involvement and commitment.

Objective 2.3: Coordinate activities between Federal, State, local, territorial, tribal, industry and other private sector partners.

Objective 2.4: Provide resources, education, training, guidance, support, and tools to partners to enable them to collaborate with and participate in IPAWS.

IPAWS' partners are divided into five major functional groups: (1) Federal Governance; (2) Federal, State, Territorial, Tribal, and Local Alerting Authorities (hereafter referred to as "Alerting Authorities"; (3) Private Sector Industry; (4) Non-Profit and Advocacy; and (5) the American People. IPAWS will conduct outreach to all partner groups and will provide targeted information for each group to: (1) detail what the partner group needs to know about IPAWS; (2) explain the benefits and detail how IPAWS is relevant to them; and (3) provide partners with opportunities, training, guidance, and tools to enable them

---

[1] Presidential Executive Order 13407, Sec 2(a)(vi-viii); June 26, 2006
[2] GAO, *Emergency Preparedness: Improved Planning and Coordination Necessary for Development of Integrated Public Alert and Warning System*, GAO-09-1044-T.
[3] Ibid.

to collaborate with and participate in IPAWS to create "an effective, reliable, integrated, flexible, and comprehensive system to alert and warn the American people."[4]

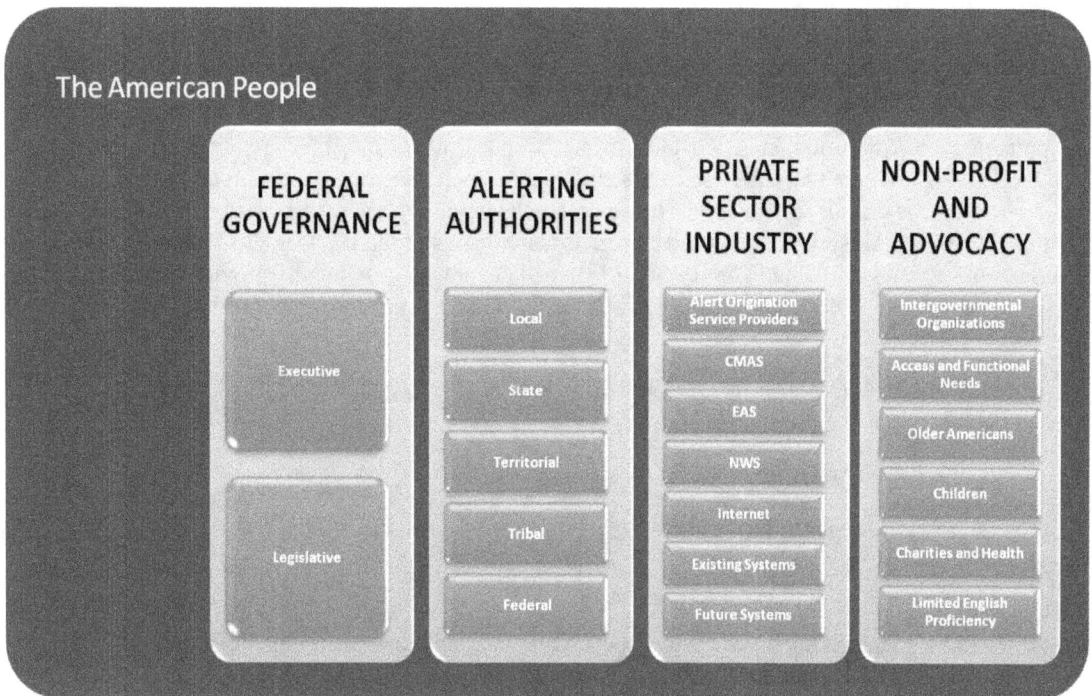

Figure 1 – The IPAWS Partner Groups

Figure 1 shows how this Outreach Plan organizes the IPAWS' partners into groups based on: (1) commonality of roles and responsibilities in public alerts and warnings; (2) similar messages and calls-to-action; and (3) the types of activities the IPAWS PMO uses to uniquely engage each partner group. The American People are the foundation of all partner groups and are the primary reason the IPAWS PMO works to create an effective, reliable, integrated, flexible, and comprehensive public alert and warning system.

---

[4] Presidential Executive Order 13047, Sec 1

1.0   COMMUNICATIONS

1.1   Messaging

It is incumbent upon the IPAWS PMO to reach out to all partners to ensure they understand how IPAWS will support the shared goal to provide timely and actionable information to ensure their safety and minimize damage to property during times of crisis.

All partners require information on what they can expect, and the actions they are expected to perform. The IPAWS PMO's core messages are consistent, but each partner group has different information needs and a one-message-fits-all approach fails to recognize the unique roles and responsibilities of each partner. Also, messages may change and evolve as components of the IPAWS PMO mature and more information becomes available. The IPAWS PMO will develop and frequently provide targeted messages for partners, including what they need to know, what they need to do, and what resources are available to them.

The IPAWS PMO will provide effective messaging to all partner groups through:

➢ Frequently communicating critical information;

➢ Facilitating an effective partner dialogue; and,

➢ Tailoring messages to incorporate diverse perspectives and information needs.

1.2   Digital Communications

Today, digital communication is key to any successful outreach initiative. Digital communications are prevalent and quickly becoming the most effective way to both share and obtain information. IPAWS will continue to invest resources to strengthen and increase digital communications for the purpose of effectively engaging a wide variety of partners.

1.2.1   Website

Between May 1, 2010 and May 1, 2011, monthly IPAWS website visits increased by 207% and hits increased by 166%. IPAWS makes a concerted effort to present relevant information as well as provide more intuitive website organization. The IPAWS PMO continually works to improve the quality, organization, relevance, and interactive nature of the information posted on the IPAWS website.

The IPAWS PMO regularly reviews old and adds new website content, with technical and communication staff working closely together to provide IPAWS partners with the best information possible. A few of the new items on the IPAWS website include information on the IPAWS PMOs adoption of components from FEMA's Disaster Management program, a calendar of events, testing information and forms, standards and protocol guidelines, accomplishments, schedules and milestones, IPAWS Program contact information, and a large archive of working group webinars. The IPAWS website is quickly becoming the place to find both high-level messaging, testing and training resources, and detailed program information.

Moving forward, IPAWS will continue to encourage partners to use the website and will:

➢ Create a link on the IPAWS homepage to an informative video, providing a comprehensive overview of IPAWS;

➢ Establish partner-specific pages to complement existing system and program-focused pages and include partner-specific education and training resources and targeted messages, including facts, key benefits, and calls-to-action;

> ➢ Refine the site organization and increase visual engagement; and,

> ➢ Make the website more interactive by adding a media library which includes IPAWS on-line training sessions, a glossary of IPAWS terms, greater detail of IPAWS' participation in conferences, demonstrations, and workshops, and a collection of best practices and case-studies.

1.2.2 eBulletin

IPAWS eBulletins will be released every other month and will be distributed through a wide variety of communications channels, although digital distribution will be the primary mechanism. Topics will rotate between specific partner groups, although a lot of content crosses multiple partner interests. While schedules of topics are planned in advance, flexibility is maintained to reflect changing events.

eBulletin content will include, but is not limited to:

> ➢ IPAWS in the News

> ➢ Technical specification details

> ➢ Recent IPAWS accomplishments

> ➢ IPAWS case-studies

> ➢ Testing and validation instructions

> ➢ Upcoming milestones, schedule, testing and training deadlines, etc.

> ➢ Information on partner events where IPAWS will participate

> ➢ Links to new training and webinars

> ➢ Best practices for originating and disseminating public alerts and warnings

> ➢ Partner-focused articles on programs of interest

1.2.3 Social Media

The IPAWS PMO will continue to work with the FEMA Web and Digital Engagement teams toward the IPAWS goals of engaging partners through an integrated set of robust social media tools, including establishing a specific IPAWS Facebook page and Twitter account.

1.3 Media Relations

IPAWS PMO staff work to craft easily understood messages for partner groups participating in specific trade media opportunities, editorial articles, expert interviews, etc. with the goal of communicating important information to partners through trade, industry, and other media publications.

1.4 Collateral Material Development

Collateral materials benefit IPAWS partners the most when they are current, targeted, and easily accessible. Rather than handing out large quantities of printed collateral materials, IPAWS makes a concerted effort to direct partners to the IPAWS website where IPAWS related information is located. The IPAWS website is a much better resource for partners than static documents.

However, fact sheets and best practices one-pagers containing actionable information and written for a specific partner group will continue to be part of the IPAWS PMO collateral material development.

Additionally, IPAWS business cards will be distributed to partners. The IPAWS business card contains the FEMA logo, IPAWS website address, IPAWS email address, ipaws@dhs.gov, and a quick response (QR) code on the back side of the card. Individuals with smart phones and a QR app will have another way to quickly and conveniently access the IPAWS website. As part of FEMA's overall preparedness initiative, IPAWS "Get Alert, Stay Alive" bags, which can be "go-bags" for emergencies, will continue to be distributed at conferences and demonstrations.

2.0 PARTNER ENGAGEMENT

2.1 Building Relationships

The IPAWS program is built upon and maintained by a strong network of relationships with both public and private sector individuals and organizations. The IPAWS PMO continuously seeks to engage partners to form relationships, share information, and receive feedback. The IPAWS PMO conducts outreach in the form of briefings, presentations, and small group meetings, to a number of partner organizations to interact with and ensure they are kept informed of IPAWS PMO progress. Working with and through them, the IPAWS PMO is able to maximize limited resources to engage large numbers of people and organizations. The objectives of smaller, individualized relationship building activities include:

- ➢ Establish dialogue with identified thought-leaders;
- ➢ Respond to partners who express a particular interest in IPAWS, ask questions, or request information or training;
- ➢ Extend invitations to individuals with expertise to participate in working groups and roundtables related to their areas of interest and expertise;

2.2 Working Groups and Roundtables

The IPAWS PMO has instituted several Working Groups and Roundtables to bring together the necessary technical and operational expertise from Federal, State, tribal, territorial and local governments, as well as private sector industry and non-profit and advocacy groups. Working Groups and Roundtable events allow partners and the IPAWS PMO to openly and collegially discuss program benefits, limitations, and solutions for emerging technologies. They establish a forum for a shared understanding of the mission, goals, and objectives. Working Groups and Roundtables also support solution-based engagement, and focus on a common goal of creating a dialogue that focuses on lessons learned, best practices, and improvement.

Working Groups and Roundtables are a very important part of IPAWS PMO outreach efforts. In addition to helping find solutions to challenges faced by IPAWS PMO partners, Working Groups and Roundtables are also used by IPAWS to clearly and frequently communicate with partners and invite partners to participate in IPAWS related activities. Organizations and individuals in the IPAWS PMO-sponsored Working Groups and Roundtables bring unique capabilities and perspectives to the table and it is through these forums that the IPAWS PMO is able to leverage the best-of-the-best, share lessons learned, and establish consensus for what needs to be done to accomplish the mission.

IPAWS currently sponsors or participates in the following Working Groups and Roundtables:

- ➢ IPAWS Federal Working Group
- ➢ IPAWS Industry Working Group
- ➢ The White House Principal Communications Working Group
- ➢ Homeland Infrastructure Foundation Level Data Working Group (HIFLD)
- ➢ Joint Special Interest Group (SIG) for Alert Disseminators
- ➢ Joint Special Interest Group (SIG) for Emergency Management Practitioners

- Americans with Access and Functional Needs Roundtable
- IPAWS and the Regional Emergency Communication Coordination Working Group (RECCWG)
- Emergency Interoperability Consortium (EIC)
- Emergency Alert System Roundtable

The IPAWS PMO coordinates with the National Communications Sector-Specific Agency and participates in Communications Government Coordinating Council activities. The IPAWS PMO is also represented on Communications Sector GCC working groups established to update the Sector Annual Report and the National Sector Risk Assessment. Finally, the IPAWS PMO will continue to expand Working Groups and Roundtables for partner groups, such as: Limited English Proficiency (LEP), Older Adults, and Alerting Authorities.

2.3   Events

Participating in events such as conferences, demonstrations, and roundtables is an important part of the IPAWS PMO outreach efforts. Events serve as a means for spreading information, engaging partners, and strengthening relationships. The Outreach Calendar of Events at Appendix B identifies opportunities for the IPAWS PMO to engage across a wide variety of partners.

Before committing to an event, IPAWS establishes a relationship with the organization's leadership to solicit and leverage the support and resources of the organization as well as identify ways the IPAWS PMO can support their event objectives. The IPAWS PMO protects limited resources by managing events efficiently and maximizes impact through effective, interactive demonstrations and on-site workshops.

2.4   Training, Demonstrations, and Exercises

The IPAWS PMO currently provides two types of technical training workshops. The Emergency Alert System (EAS) and Common Alerting Protocol (CAP) Workshops are tailored to Private Sector Industry. Both workshops provide an interactive discussion of EAS-CAP equipment, including installation, configuration, and operation as well as a live demonstration. The workshops also provide information on technical challenges facing EAS Participants and a discussion of various mitigation strategies to resolve issues. Additionally, and in partnership with FEMA's Emergency Management Institute, IPAWS will continue to develop workshops and training courses for Alerting Authorities.

The IPAWS PMO conducts frequent demonstrations of IPAWS' proof of concept end-to-end operations, including alert origination, alert aggregation (using the IPAWS Open Platform for Emergency Networks, or IPAWS OPEN), and alert dissemination technologies for partners. IPAWS collaborates with numerous partners during these demonstrations to increase the impact and scope of the demonstrations.

The IPAWS PMO is also required to conduct table-top, scenario-based, and full scale exercises of public alert and warning communication systems. IPAWS works closely with Private Sector Industry and Federal, State, Tribal, Territorial, and Local Alerting Authorities to identify gaps, capture best practices and lessons learned, and implement mitigation strategies. IPAWS also engages media to help communicate with and prepare the American people for these exercises.

2.5   Standards Testing

IPAWS PMO actively conducts outreach to Private Sector Industry partners to encourage and facilitate testing of alert and warning technologies against nationally and internationally established standards and protocols. IPAWS provides partners with testing information, instructions, forms, and testing facilities.

The IPAWS Demonstration and Test (D&T) Center at the Joint Interoperability Test Command provides Private Sector Industry a chance to test EAS-CAP equipment in a live environment. Additionally, future alert and warning technologies that use the OPEN platform will be integrated into the testing at the IPAWS D&T Center.

The IPAWS PMO will continue to increase outreach efforts to Private Sector Industry partners and provide them with information and resources they need to test their technologies and to ensure greater interoperability with the IPAWS Open Platform for Emergency Networks.

3.0   TARGETED MESSAGES FOR PARTNERS

3.1   Key Talking Points

These talking points can be used when engaging all IPAWS partners:

- ➢ The Integrated Public Alert and Warning System (IPAWS) is the nation's next-generation infrastructure of alert and warning networks.

- ➢ The IPAWS expands upon the traditional audio-only radio and television Emergency Alert System (EAS) by providing one message over more devices to more people before, during, and after a crisis so they may take mitigating actions to save lives and reduce damage to property

- ➢ In 2006, Executive Order 13407 gave DHS the responsibility for modernizing the public alert and warning system; DHS charged FEMA with this responsibility

- ➢ The vision of IPAWS is to provide "Timely Alert and Warning to the American People in the preservation of life and property"

- ➢ The IPAWS ensures that the President can send alert and warning messages to the public under all conditions

- ➢ The IPAWS will provide Federal, State, territorial, tribal, and local warning authorities the capabilities to alert and warn their respective communities of all hazards impacting public safety and well-being via multiple communications pathways.

- ➢ FEMA is on schedule to achieve our IPAWS vision in fiscal year 2012. Meeting that schedule means four things:

  - o IPAWS will have interoperable standards and interfaces in place

  - o IPAWS will have redundancy built into the dissemination network

  - o IPAWS will have integrated disparate message distribution paths, meaning that one message can travel many paths to reach the American public

  - o IPAWS will increase the number of PEP stations to provide additional direct coverage of EAS

- ➢ The IPAWS is designed to accommodate public alerting systems that may not have been invented yet

3.2   The American People

Facts: What the American People need to know:

1) When disasters strike, whether they are natural, accidental, or man-made, it has always been vital that alerts and warnings be reported accurately and in a timely fashion to those who may be in danger.

2) It is the policy of the United States to have an effective, reliable, integrated, flexible, and comprehensive system to alert and warn the American people.

3) Integrated Public Alert and Warning System, or IPAWS, is the solution for effective public alerts and warnings.

4) IPAWS allows alerting authorities to write their own message using open standards. The message is then authenticated by the IPAWS Open Platform for Emergency Networks -- or OPEN-- to be delivered simultaneously through multiple communications devices reaching as many people as possible to save lives and protect property.

5) IPAWS must ensure the President can reach the American people, but the IPAWS PMO recognizes that most alerts and warnings are issued at a state and local level.

6) IPAWS alerts and warnings are location-specific and therefore more relevant to those receiving the alert.

7) Through the use of open standards such as the Common Alert Protocol, IPAWS allows for growth and integration with future consumer technologies.

8) In addition to the President, alerting authorities include State, local, territorial, and tribal public safety officials who are designated within their level of government as an authority responsible for communicating emergency alerts and warnings to the public.

9) After completing FEMA-sponsored training, alerting authorities will be authenticated for access to IPAWS. They will then be able to use Common Alerting Protocol compliant emergency and incident management tools to create location-specific alerts that are scaled to cover areas as big as their entire jurisdiction or a much smaller area within their jurisdiction. Once created, the alert will then be sent to IPAWS OPEN.

10) Once the alert is received from the alerting authorities, IPAWS OPEN authenticates the source and validates that the alert input conforms to the Common Alerting Protocol standard and IPAWS profile. This provides a standard for everyone across all levels of government as well as the private sector.

11) While older systems relied on audio and text-only systems, IPAWS-OPEN makes picture and video feeds possible and allows for the seamless incorporation of emerging technologies.

12) Emergency alerts will be delivered across multiple pathways to the American people.

13) Alerts will be delivered by the Emergency Alert System, using AM, FM, and satellite radio as well as broadcast, cable, and satellite TV.

14) The Personal Localized Alerting Network (PLAN), technically known as the Commercial Mobile Alert System (CMAS) will send alerts to cell phones and other commercial mobile network devices based on their location, even if cellular networks are overloaded and can no longer support calls, text, and emails.

15) State, local, territorial, and tribal alerting systems such as emergency telephone networks, giant voice sirens, and digital road signs may also receive alerts from IPAWS-OPEN and future alerting technologies and systems can be easily integrated into the IPAWS.

16) When disaster strikes, the IPAWS allows emergency managers and alerting authorities at all levels to send one message to more people over more devices, to save lives and protect property.

17) No matter where you are: at home, at school, at work, or even on vacation, you can get life-saving alerts.

Key Benefits: Why the American People want to know the facts:

1) Alerting authorities will send life-saving information to the American People before, during, and after a crisis.

2) IPAWS alerts and warnings are location specific and, therefore, more relevant to those receiving the alert.

Calls-to-Action: What the American People need to do:

1) Respond appropriately to instructions from alerting authorities and public officials once an alert or warning has been issued.

3.3 Federal Governance Partners

Federal Governance Partners are Federal authorities who are responsible for national policies and regulations affecting public alerts and warnings.

Facts: What Federal Governance Partners need to know:

1) In 2006, Executive Order 13407 gave DHS the responsibility for modernizing the public alert and warning system; DHS charged FEMA with this responsibility.

2) IPAWS ensures that the President can send alert and warn messages to the public under all conditions.

3) IPAWS will provide Federal, State, territorial, tribal, and local warning authorities the capabilities to alert and warn their respective communities of all hazards impacting public safety and well-being via multiple communications pathways.

4) The IPAWS PMO is implementing a proactive partner communications outreach plan to support State, local, tribal, and territorial interest and use of IPAWS.

Key Benefits: Why Federal Governance Partners want to know the facts:

1) Alerting authorities will be able to send life-saving information to the American People before, during, and after a crisis.

2) IPAWS ensures the President or the President's designee, can send alert and warn messages to the public under all conditions.

Calls-to-Action: What Federal Governance Partners need to do:

1) Collaborate with the IPAWS PMO and IPAWS' partners to promote policies, regulations, and guidelines which will facilitate the development, implementation, and adoption of an effective, reliable, integrated, flexible, and comprehensive alert and warning system.

2) Continue to dedicate resources to support and sustain IPAWS' two major components, the Primary Entry Point Modernization and Expansion Program (PEP Program) and the IPAWS Open Platform for Emergency Networks (IPAWS OPEN), as well as a number of other initiatives undertaken by IPAWS.

3) Participate in working groups for IPAWS Federal Governance partners.

3.4 Federal, State, Local, Tribal, and Territorial Alerting Authorities

Alerting Authorities at the Federal, State, local, tribal, and territorial levels are the individuals authorized to send alert and warning messages to their respective communities.

Facts: What Alerting Authorities Need to know:

1) Alerting Authorities will use Alert Origination Service Provider tools to send alerts to IPAWS OPEN, which will then be simultaneously distributed across multiple communication pathways.

2) Public Alerting Systems facilitated by the IPAWS include: the Emergency Alert System (EAS) (which is being modernized and expanded); PLAN/CMAS; National Weather Service's family of alert dissemination services, including NOAA Weather Radio; Internet; unique and local alerting systems; and can incorporate future technologies.

3) PLAN/CMAS is scheduled to launch in 2011. When deployed, it will provide Alerting Authorities with the ability to send alerts to mobile devices in targeted geographic areas.

4) IPAWS is working with private sector industry partners to make their alert technologies work with IPAWS-OPEN; examples include: telephone, text and email notification, devices and services for people with disabilities, Internet, digital signage, and future communications tools that become commonplace for public use.

5) Alerting Authorities will need to be authenticated to use the IPAWS system. The application process for IPAWS Alerting Authorities will be determined by individual States, tribes, and territories.

6) Alerting Authorities will be required to attend on-line training before accessing IPAWS-OPEN; on-line training will be made available through the Emergency Management Institute (EMI).

7) There is no charge for Alerting Authorities to access the IPAWS system.

8) The IPAWS PMO is implementing a proactive partner communications outreach plan to support State, local, tribal, and territorial interest and use of IPAWS.

9) After completing FEMA-sponsored training, alerting authorities will be authenticated for access to IPAWS. They will then be able to use Common Alerting Protocol compliant emergency and incident management tools to create location-specific alerts that are scaled to cover areas as big as their entire jurisdiction or a much smaller area within their jurisdiction. Once created, the alert will then be sent to IPAWS OPEN.

10) Once the alert is received from the alerting authorities, IPAWS OPEN authenticates the source and validates that the alert input conforms to the Common Alerting Protocol standard and IPAWS profile. This provides a standard for everyone across all levels of government as well as the private sector.

11) Once the alert message has been authenticated by IPAWS-OPEN, the message is simultaneously delivered to all IPAWS-compliant public alerting systems.

Key Benefits: Why Alerting Authorities want to know the facts:

1) IPAWS will provide new communication pathways to alert and warn the local public in order to enhance public safety.

2) IPAWS is designed to address the reality that individual communication preferences change rapidly.

3) PLAN/CMAS will mitigate the difficult challenges of convincing the public to sign up to receive alerts through mobile devices.

4) Access to IPAWS is available to Alerting Authorities at no cost.

Calls-to-Action: What Alerting Authorities need to do:

1) Watch for information on how Alerting Authorities can be authenticated to use IPAWS.

2) Participate in IPAWS on-line training through FEMA's Emergency Management Institute.

3) Incorporate IPAWS into local activities such as:

    a. Response plans and procedures;

    b. Training and exercises; and,

    c. Public outreach campaigns, including school and university programs.

4) Support the use of the Common Alerting Protocol (CAP) and national and international standards and procedures as adopted by the IPAWS PMO.

5) Participate in working groups for IPAWS Alerting Authorities.

3.5 Private Sector Industry Partners

Alert Origination Tool Providers produce technology, tools, and software applications that can be used by Alerting Authorities to create and send alert messages.

Public Alerting System Providers are those who make technology available to distribute alert and warning messages to the public. They are generally commercial organizations, including EAS participants, commercial mobile service providers, and internet service providers. They can also be a government agency such as the National Weather Service.

Facts: What Private Sector Industry Partners need to know:

1) The IPAWS mission is to provide integrated services and capabilities to Alerting Authorities that enable them to alert and warn their communities via multiple communication pathways.

2) IPAWS will provide Federal, State, territorial, tribal, and local warning authorities the capabilities to alert and warn their respective communities of all hazards impacting public safety and well-being via multiple communications pathways.

3) IPAWS supports Presidential messaging capability.

4) Alerting Authorities will use Alert Origination Service Provider tools to send alerts to IPAWS OPEN, which will then be simultaneously distributed across multiple communication pathways.

5) To ensure interoperability with IPAWS OPEN, alert and warning technologies will need to meet certain standards and accommodate protocols such as the CAP.

6) Guidelines for Private Sector Industry alerting technologies to be interoperable with IPAWS can be obtained on the IPAWS website, www.fema.gov/emergency/ipaws.

7) Investments made by IPAWS Private Sector Industry partners will help protect lives and property.

8) The IPAWS program office is implementing a proactive partner communications outreach plan to support State, local, tribal, and territorial interest and the use of the IPAWS.

Key Benefits: Why Private Sector Industry Partners want to know the facts:

1) As partners embrace IPAWS, demand is likely to grow for commercial notification technologies and services that work within the IPAWS program.

2) There is no fee for Private Sector Partners to integrate with IPAWS-OPEN.

3) Using standards and protocols adopted by IPAWS, Private Sector Industry partners can ensure their alert and warning technology is interoperable with IPAWS.

4) IPAWS helps save lives and protect property.

Calls-to-Action: What Private Sector Industry Partners need to do:

1) Use standards and protocols adopted by IPAWS when developing alert and warning technologies.

2) Become familiar with standards, processes, testing procedures, agreements, etc. that make participation with IPAWS possible.

3) Partner with IPAWS in assisting with outreach to State, local, tribal, and territorial governments, as well as the American people.

4) Participate in working groups for IPAWS Private Sector Industry partners.

3.5.1 Private Sector Industry Partner Sub-Messages: Alert Origination Service Providers

Facts: What Alert Origination Service Providers need to know:

1) To ensure interoperability with IPAWS-OPEN, Alert Origination Service Providers will need to meet certain standards and accommodate protocols such as the CAP.

2) Alert origination services will need to undergo testing to demonstrate conformity to IPAWS standards and protocols.

Key Benefits: Why Alert Origination Service Providers want to know the facts:

1) Alert Origination Service Providers can be incorporated and interoperable with IPAWS-OPEN through compliance with IPAWS standards and protocols.

Calls-to-Action: What Alert Origination Service Providers need to do:

1) Keep informed of opportunities related to IPAWS.

2) Keep informed of conformity testing requirements and opportunities.

3) Participate in working groups for IPAWS Alert Origination Service Provider partners.

3.5.2 Private Sector Industry Partner Sub-Messages: PLAN/CMAS Participants

PLAN/CMAS Carriers are the commercial cellular providers who have chosen to participate in PLAN/CMAS in accordance with federal regulations.

Facts: What PLAN/CMAS Participants need to know:

1) PLAN/CMAS supports Presidential messaging capability, imminent threat alerts and warnings, and AMBER alerts.

2) State, local, tribal, and territorial authorities are interested in and excited about the possibilities of using PLAN/CMAS for alerts and warnings.

3) The IPAWS PMO is implementing a proactive partner communications outreach plan to enhance State, local, tribal and territorial interest and use of PLAN/CMAS technology.

Key Benefits: Why PLAN/CMAS Participants want to know the facts:

1) PLAN/CMAS participants help create a new important means of protecting lives and property.

2) It is anticipated that demand for commercial notification services will be created.

Calls-to-Action: What PLAN/CMAS Participants need to do:

1) Continue technology development to meet PLAN/CMAS requirements.

2) Partner with IPAWS in assisting with outreach to State, local, tribal, and territorial governments, as well as the American people.

3) Comply with regulatory requirements established by the FCC.

4) Participate in working groups for IPAWS' Commercial Alert Service Provider partners.

3.5.3 Private Sector Industry Partner Sub-Messages: EAS Participants

EAS participants are entities required under the Commission's rules to comply with EAS rules, *e.g.* , analog radio and television stations, and wired and wireless cable television systems, DBS, DTV, SDARS, digital cable and DAB, and wireline video systems.[5]

EAS Vendors are private companies engaged in commercial endeavors to make equipment and software available to transmit and receive EAS messages. While the EAS Vendor industry has been around for years, it is undergoing material changes because of EAS initiatives.

Facts: What EAS Participants need to know:

1) A national test of the EAS system will take place late 2011.

2) Per FCC regulations, EAS decoders/encoders are required to meet certain standards and accommodate protocols such as the CAP.

3) EAS decoders/encoders need to undergo testing to demonstrate conformity to IPAWS standards and protocols.

4) IPAWS is modernizing and enhancing the EAS: EAS enhancements include:

   a. Expansion of and improvements to Primary Entry Point (PEP) stations;

   b. Digitization of EAS sending and receiving equipment, which will require technology upgrades for EAS participants; and,

   c. Adoption of standards (such as CAP) that will help facilitate alert communication.

Key Benefits: Why EAS Participants want to know the facts:

1) An improved EAS system will help solidify EAS participants' position as a popular and reliable source of emergency information for the public.

2) Proper EAS participation helps satisfy regulatory requirements.

3) EAS is and will remain an integral part of IPAWS.

4) EAS enhancement efforts provide a strong opportunity for EAS participants to strengthen relationships with local public safety officials.

5) EAS helps save lives and protect property.

Calls-to-Action: What EAS Participants need to do:

1) Keep informed of regulations and opportunities related to EAS enhancements.

2) Keep informed of conformity testing requirements and opportunities.

3) Upgrade EAS equipment prior to FCC deadlines.

4) Prepare for the National EAS Test, including helping to prepare the public.

5) Participate in the IPAWS Emergency Alert System Roundtable.

---

[5] CFR 47 Part 11

3.5.4 Private Sector Industry Partner Sub-Messages: Internet Service Providers

Facts: What Internet Service Providers need to know:

1) To ensure interoperability with IPAWS-OPEN, internet services will need to meet certain standards and accommodate protocols such as the CAP.

2) Internet services will need to undergo testing to demonstrate conformity to the IPAWS standards and protocols.

3) Internet Service Providers can help create a new, important means for protecting lives and property.

Key Benefits: Why Internet Service Providers want to know the facts:

1) Internet service alert and warning technologies can be incorporated and interoperable with IPAWS-OPEN through compliance with IPAWS standards and protocols.

2) It is anticipated that internet alert and warning services will be widely used.

3) State, local, tribal, and territorial authorities are interested in and excited about the possibilities of using internet services for alerts and warnings.

Calls-to-Action: What Internet Service Providers need to do:

1) Keep informed of opportunities related to the IPAWS.

2) Keep informed of conformity testing requirements and opportunities.

3) Participate in working groups for the IPAWS Internet Service Provider partners.

3.5.5 Private Sector Industry Partner Sub-Messages: Unique and Local Alerting System Providers

Facts: What Unique and Local Alerting System Providers need to know:

1) To ensure interoperability with IPAWS-OPEN, unique and local alerting systems will need to meet certain standards and accommodate protocols such as the CAP.

2) Unique and local alerting systems will need to undergo testing to demonstrate conformity to IPAWS standards and protocols.

Key Benefits: Why Unique and Local Alerting System Providers want to know the facts:

1) Unique and local alerting systems can be incorporated and interoperable with IPAWS-OPEN through compliance with the IPAWS standards and protocols.

2) State, local, tribal, and territorial authorities are interested in and excited about the possibilities of integrating unique and local alerting systems into a broad network of communication pathways.

Calls-to-Action: What Unique and Local Alerting System Providers need to do:

1) Keep informed of opportunities related to the IPAWS.

2) Keep informed of conformity testing requirements and opportunities.

3) Participate in working groups for IPAWS Unique and Local Alerting System Provider partners.

3.5.6 Private Sector Industry Partner Sub-Messages: Future Alerting Technology Developers

Facts: What Future Alert Technology Developers need to know:

1) To ensure interoperability with IPAWS-OPEN, future alerting systems will need to meet certain standards and accommodate protocols such as the CAP.

2) Future alerting systems will need to undergo testing to demonstrate conformity to the IPAWS standards and protocols.

Key Benefits: Why Future Alert Technology Developers want to know the facts:

1) Future alerting systems can be incorporated and interoperable with IPAWS-OPEN through compliance with IPAWS standards and protocols.

2) State, local, tribal, and territorial authorities are interested in and excited about the possibilities of integrating future alerting systems into a broad network of communication pathways.

Calls-to-Action: What Future Alert Technology Developers need to do:

1) Keep informed of opportunities related to the IPAWS.

2) Keep informed of conformity testing requirements and opportunities.

3) Participate in working groups for the IPAWS Private Sector Industry partners.

3.6 Non-Profit and Advocacy Partners

Facts: What Non-Profit and Advocacy Partners need to know:

1) In 2006, Executive Order 13407 gave DHS the responsibility for modernizing the public alert and warning system; DHS charged FEMA with this responsibility.

2) The IPAWS ensures that the President can send alert and warning messages to the public under all conditions.

3) The IPAWS will provide Federal, State, territorial, tribal, and local warning authorities the capabilities to alert and warn their respective communities of all hazards impacting public safety and well-being via multiple communication pathways.

4) Executive Order requires the IPAWS to "include in the public alert and warning system the capability to alert and warn all Americans, including those with disabilities and those without an understanding of the English language."[6]

5) The IPAWS PMO is implementing a proactive partner communications outreach plan to support State, local, tribal, and territorial interest and the use of the IPAWS.

Key Benefits: Why Non-Profit and Advocacy Partners want to know the facts:

1) Alerting authorities will be able to send life-saving information to the American People before, during, and after a crisis.

2) The IPAWS ensures that the President, or the President's designee, can send alert and warning messages to the public under all conditions.

Calls-to-Action: What Non-Profit and Advocacy Partners need to do:

1) Collaborate with the IPAWS PMO to identify best practices for alerts and warnings.

---

[6] Executive Order 13407 Section 2(a)(iv)

2) Assist the IPAWS PMO in engaging partners with interests in the development, implementation, and adoption of an effective, reliable, integrated, flexible, and comprehensive alert and warning system.

3) Participate in working groups for the IPAWS Non-Profit and Advocacy partners.

SUMMARY

FEMA's IPAWS PMO is the leading federal organization ensuring the President of the United States has the capability to address the American people under all conditions. IPAWS integrates current and future alerting technologies and encourages interoperability of systems through common protocols and standards while making these technologies and capabilities available to alerting authorities across all levels of government.

Outreach activities, strategic communications, and partner engagement are becoming increasingly targeted, robust, and accelerated as the IPAWS matures and achieves important milestones. The full potential of IPAWS cannot be realized without the many partners involved in public alert and warnings and the IPAWS PMO remains committed to and actively engaged with partners to achieve our shared goal to save lives and protect property.

APPENDIX A: ORGANIZATIONS FOR OUTREACH TARGETING

The IPAWS PMO has categorized partners into five major functional groups: (1) Federal Governance; (2) Federal, State, Territorial, Tribal, and Local Alerting Authorities, or "Alerting Authorities"; (3) Private Sector Industry; (4) Non-Profit and Advocacy; and (5) the American People. There are many organizations and interest groups within each of these partner groups, many of which IPAWS actively engages. The list below is a broad, but not an exhaustive, list of current or future partner organizations the IPAWS PMO would like to engage.

FEDERAL GOVERNANCE PARTNERS

Government partner organizations are also important to the success of the IPAWS program. They represent a large and unique segment of the emergency management community and the American public.

Federal Executive Government Partners

- The White House, Executive Office of the President
- Department of Defense (DOD)
- DOD Joint Interoperability Test Command (JITC)
- Department of Homeland Security (DHS)
- DHS Cyber Security and Telecommunications
- DHS Executive Leaderships
- DHS Office of Civil Liberties, Civil Rights, and Children's Working Group
- DHS Operations
- DHS Policy
- DHS Science and Technology
- Federal Communications Commission (FCC)
- FCC Public Safety and Homeland Security Bureau (PSHSB)
- Federal Emergency Management Agency (FEMA)
- FEMA Acquisition Program Office (APO)
- FEMA Emergency Management Institute
- FEMA Executive Leadership
- FEMA Office of External Affairs
- FEMA Office of Disability Integration and Coordination (ODIC)
- FEMA Regional Communications Coordinators Working Group (RECCWG)
- National Oceanic and Atmospheric Administration (NOAA)
- National Weather Service (NWS)
- NOAA Region External Affairs
- Department of Justice (DOJ)
- National Security Council (NSC)

- State, Local, Tribal, and Territorial Government Coordinating Council (SLTTGCC)
- Critical Infrastructure Partnership Advisory Council (CIPAC)
- IPAWS Federal Working Group

Legislative Government Partners

The IPAWS PMO has engaged with Congressional Committees who have legislative oversight of IPAWS. Quarterly reports are provided to these committees and IPAWS PMO leadership regularly engage with key members of these committees to provide updates on IPAWS implementation. IPAWS also conducted an interactive end-to-end IPAWS concept of operations demonstration for members of Congress and their staff at the US Capitol Visitors Center.

US Congress:

- United States Senate Committee on Appropriations
- United States Senate Committee on Homeland Security and Governmental Affairs
- United States House of Representatives Committee on Transportation and Infrastructure
- United States House of Representatives Committee on Appropriations
- United States House of Representatives Subcommittee on Economic Development, Public Buildings, and Emergency Management
- United States House of Representatives Subcommittee on Emergency Communications, Preparedness, and Response

Federal, State, Territorial, Tribal, and State Alerting Authorities Partners

In addition to the President, alerting authorities include State, local, territorial, and tribal public safety officials who are designated within their level of government as an authority responsible for communicating emergency alerts and warnings to the public.

- IPAWS Originator Practitioners' Working Group (OPWG)
- International Association of Emergency Managers (IAEM)
- National Emergency Managers Association (NEMA)
- Association of Public Safety Communications Officials (APCO)
- Community Emergency Preparedness Information Network (CEPIN)
- International Association of Chiefs of Police (IACP)
- International Association of Fire Chiefs
- National Emergency Number Association (NENA)
- Regional Emergency Communications Coordination Working Group (RECCWG)
- State Emergency Communications Committees (SECC)
- State Homeland Security and Emergency Management Offices
- The Weather Channel
- U.S. First Responders Association
- Various Urban Area Security Initiatives (UASIs)

PRIVATE SECTOR INDUSTRY PARTNERS

Private Sector Industry partners are comprised of representatives from private sector companies with recognized equities in the alert and warning field. Since the majority of the infrastructure needed to accomplish the IPAWS mission is owned and operated by the private sector, the private sector is a key partner in the development and implementation of IPAWS.

Alert Origination Service Providers

➢ Emergency Interoperability Consortium

Dissemination Groups

➢ IPAWS Disseminator Practitioners' Working Group (DPWG)

➢ Alliance for Access to Technology

➢ American Cable Association

➢ Association of Public Television Stations

➢ AT&T Services, Inc.

➢ Cellular Telecommunications and Internet Association—The Wireless Association (CTIA)

➢ EAS-CAP Industry Group

➢ Latino Public Radio Consortium

➢ National Alliance of State Broadcasters Associations (NASBA)

➢ National Association of Broadcasters (NAB)

➢ National Cable and Telecommunications Association

➢ National Federation of Community Broadcasters (NFCB)

➢ National Public Radio (NPR)

➢ Public Broadcasting Service (PBS)

➢ Satellite Broadcast & Communications Association (SBCA)

➢ Society of Broadcast Engineers (SBE)

➢ Society of Cable Telecommunications Engineers (SCTE)

➢ State Chapter Broadcaster/Cable/Satellite Associations

➢ Telecommunications Industry Association

➢ Telecommunications Sector Government Coordinating Council (GCC)

➢ Primary Entry Point Advisory Committee (PEPAC)

NON-PROFIT AND ADVOCACY PARTNERS

The IPAWS PMO continuously seeks to engage with new partners to form relationships, share information, and receive feedback. The IPAWS PMO conducts outreach and engages a number of intra-governmental, non-profit, and advocacy organizations to ensure they are kept informed of IPAWS progress.

Additionally, Executive Order 13407 specifically requires IPAWS to, "include in the public alert and warning system the capability to alert and warn all Americans, including those with disabilities and those without an understanding of the English language."

Intra-Governmental Organizations

Engagement with intra-governmental organizations will initially focus on making senior leaders aware of IPAWS goals and objectives. Each organization, with the exception of the Council of State Governments has an office in Washington, DC. After engaging with the organizations' leaders, IPAWS will seek participation in various meetings and conferences to maximize the exposure of IPAWS to the very broad membership base in each organization. The IPAWS PMO will coordinate with each organization to determine the level of participation and engagement that IPAWS leadership can expect.

- ➤ The Council of State Governments (CSG)
- ➤ The International City/County Management Association (ICMA)
- ➤ National Academy of Public Administration (NAPA)
- ➤ National Association of Counties (NACo)
- ➤ National Conference of State Legislatures (NCSL)
- ➤ National Governor's Association
- ➤ National League of Cities (NLC)
- ➤ National Congress of American Indians (NCAI)

ADA/People with Access and Functional Needs

- ➤ National Federation of the Blind
- ➤ National Association of the Deaf
- ➤ American Association of People with Disabilities/Coalition of Organizations for Accessible Technology (AAPD/COAT)
- ➤ The Coalition of Organizations for Accessible Technology (AAPD/COAT)
- ➤ Consortium for Citizens with Disabilities and the National Disability Rights Network
- ➤ Deaf Link
- ➤ Gallaudet University
- ➤ Georgia Tech Center for Advanced Communications Policy
- ➤ Hearing, Speech & Deafness Center
- ➤ Interagency Coordinating Council on Emergency Preparedness and Individuals with Disabilities
- ➤ Massachusetts Statewide Independent Living Council
- ➤ National Adult Protective Services Association
- ➤ National Association of Councils on Developmental Disabilities
- ➤ National Institute on Disability and Rehabilitation Research (NIDRR)
- ➤ National Organization on Disability/Emergency Preparedness Initiative
- ➤ SPECIAL INTEREST GROUPNTEL (Horace Mann School of the Deaf / Boston Mass)
- ➤ National Center for Accessible Media (NCAM)
- ➤ National Council on Independent Living (NCIL)
- ➤ National Council on Disability (NCD)
- ➤ National Disability Rights Network
- ➤ University of Kansas (Life Span Institute/ Research and Training on Independent Living)
- ➤ United States Access Board
- ➤ WGBH National Center for Accessible Media
- ➤ World Institute on Disability

Older Americans

- American Association of Homes and Services for the Aging (AAHSA)
- National Association of Area Agencies on Aging (n4a)
- National Association of States United for Aging and Disability (NASUAD)
- National Council on Aging

Children

- National Center for Missing & Exploited Children

Charities and Health

- American Health Care Association
- National Association of State Mental Health Program Directors (NASMHPD
- US Red Cross

Standards Based Organizations

- Organization for the Advancement of Structured Information Standards (OASIS)
- IEEE Advancing Technology for Humanity

Limited English Proficiency

- National Limited English Proficient (LEP) Advocacy Task Force
- LEP Advocacy Interpreter Standards Committee

THE AMERICAN PEOPLE

- The American People
- Media

The IPAWS PMO hosts and participates in a wide variety of events and activities where IPAWS PMO staff can engage partners on our shared goal to save lives and protect property through timely, effective public alerts and warnings.

Since January 2010, the IPAWS PMO has participated in over 100 events and activities which have engaged Americans across all IPAWS partner groups. Moving forward, the IPAWS PMO will continue to engage partners through events, conferences, meetings, roundtables, working groups, etc. The activities listed below are representative of the various kinds of activities IPAWS has or will host and/or participate in with alert and warning partners.

Month/Year	Event/Activity	Partner Group
January 2010	Alaska EAS Exercise	Alerting Authorities Private Sector Industry Federal Governance American People
	DM-OPEN Joint Special Interest Group teleconference	Private Sector Industry
	Harvard NPLI group--FEMA and EM nation-wide project	Alerting Authorities
February 2010	Technologies for Critical Preparedness (TCIP) Conference	Private Sector Industry
	Regional Call (RECCWG) to Region Two	Alerting Authorities
	NAB (NASBA) EAS National Summit	Private Sector Industry
March 2010	Regional Call (RECCWG) to Region Two	Alerting Authorities
	National Emergency Management Association (NEMA) Mid-Year Meeting	Alerting Authorities
	Association of Public Safety Communications Officials	Alerting Authorities
	National Emergency Number Association 911 Conference	Alerting Authorities
	CMAS Joint Live Meeting	Private Sector Industry
	Satellite 2010	Private Sector Industry
	Continuity of Operations Strategic Planning Conference	Federal Governance
	IPAWS briefing to DIIS CIO	Federal Governance
	Region Two DEC meeting	Alerting Authorities
	CTIA—The Wireless Association Annual Conference	Private Sector Industry
	Region 9 RECCWG	Alerting Authorities
	National Hurricane Conference	Alerting Authorities
April 2010	Region 4 RECCWG	Alerting Authorities
	National Association of Broadcasters Annual Show 2010	Private Sector Industry
	NDIA 11th Annual Science & Engineering Technology Conference	Private Sector Industry
	Maryland Mass Casualty Exercise on Light Rail System	Private Sector Industry Federal Governance American People
	Region 8 RECCWG	Alerting Authorities
May 2010	New Jersey Emergency Preparedness Workshop	Alerting Authorities
	Maryland IMT Exercise for Simulated Tornado	Alerting Authorities
	Region 1 RECCWG Plenary	Alerting Authorities
	IPAWS Conference Calls to Regions	Alerting Authorities
	National Association of Government Communicators (NAGC)	Non-Profit and Advocacy

Month/Year	Event/Activity	Partner Group
May 2010 (cont.)	National Association of Counties (NACo) (Regional Meeting)	Non-Profit and Advocacy
	Council of State Governments Spring Conference	Non-Profit and Advocacy
	Florida Governor's Hurricane Conference	Alerting Authorities Federal Governance
	DHS S&T Stakeholders Conference-East	Federal Governance
	Great Lakes HS Regional Training Conf/Expo	Alerting Authorities
June 2010	Region 5 RECCWG	Alerting Authorities
	National Emergency Number (911) Conf and Expo	Alerting Authorities
	World Conference on Disaster Management	Alerting Authorities
	FCC EAS/IPAWS workshop	Private Sector Industry Federal Governance
	IAEM Mid-year meeting	Alerting Authorities Private Sector Industry
	U. S. Conference of Mayors	Non-Profit and Advocacy
	Emergency Interoperability Consortium (EIC) meeting	Private Sector Industry
	NOAA NWS Partners Meeting	Alerting Authorities Federal Governance
	CSEPP National Workshop & Kentucky Governor's Emergency Management Workshop	Alerting Authorities Federal Governance
July 2010	Americans with Access and Special Functional Needs-IPAWS/OCIC Roundtable	Non-Profit and Advocacy
	National Association of Counties (NACo) Annual Conference and Expo	Non-Profit and Advocacy
	National Council for Independent Living (NCIL) (ADA 20th Anniversary) Annual Conference	Non-Profit and Advocacy
	Joint Special Interest Group for Emergency Manager Practitioners and Developers webinar	Private Sector Industry
August 2010	DM-Framework/Practitioner Special Interest Group	Alerting Authorities
	IPAWS Quarterly Conference Calls to RECCWG	Alerting Authorities
	Oklahoma Emergency Managers State Conference	Alerting Authorities
	Ribbon cutting ceremony: Jacksonville, FL PEP	Private Sector Industry American People
September 2010	National Capitol Region Interoperability Council CIOS	Federal Governance
	Table Top Exercise: EAS	Private Sector Industry
	Region Three RECCWG Conference	Alerting Authorities
	Congressional Demonstration	Federal Governance
	Northwest Tribal Conference	Non-Profit and Advocacy
	One DHS Day on the Hill	Federal Governance American People
	Latino Leadership Summit	Non-Profit and Advocacy
	NAB Radio Show	Private Sector Industry
October 2010	Regional Baltimore Urban Area Security Initiative Conference	Alerting Authorities
	Connecticut Association of Broadcasters Meeting	Private Sector Industry
	White House meeting: EAS Test	Federal Governance
	NEMA Emergency Managers Annual Conference	Alerting Authorities
	The White House Principal Communications Working Group	Federal Governance
	NOAA US/ Canada Face to Face on CAP	Private Sector Industry Executive Leadership

Month/Year	Event/Activity	Partner Group
October 2010 (cont.)	International Association of Emergency Managers and EMEX (Annual)	Alerting Authorities Private Sector Industry
November 2010	IPAWS Quarterly Conference calls to RECCWG	Alerting Authorities
	HIFLD Homeland Infrastructure Foundation Level Data Working Group	Federal Governance
	NOAA Technology Summit	Private Sector Industry Federal Governance
	Alaska Broadcasting Association Conference	Private Sector Industry
	National Congress of American Indians Annual Conference	Non-Profit and Advocacy
	IPAWS briefing in Virgin Islands	Alerting Authorities
	Arizona Emergency Managers Conference	Alerting Authorities
	National Public Safety Telecommunications Council (NPSTC)	Private Sector Industry
	National League of Cities Congress of Cities and Expo	Non-Profit and Advocacy
December 2010	Primary Entry Point Meeting	Private Sector Industry
	Regional Urban Area Security Initiative Conference	Alerting Authorities
January 2011	Consumer Electronic Trade Show	Private Sector Industry
	IPAWS Quarterly Conference calls to RECCWG	Alerting Authorities
	Joint Special Interest Group Emergency Management Practitioners webinar	Alerting Authorities
	AFCCE Meeting	Private Sector Industry
	Joint Special Interest Group Disseminators webinar	Private Sector Industry
	Alaska EAS Test	Private Sector Industry
	Joint Special Interest Group Emergency Management Practitioners webinar	Alerting Authorities
February 2011	IAEM Special Needs Committee Meeting	Alerting Authorities Non-Profit and Advocacy
	IPAWS Americans with Access and Functional Needs Roundtable	Private Sector Industry Non-Profit and Advocacy
	Congressional Briefings	Federal Governance
	National Continuity Programs' EAS-CAP Town Hall	Private Sector Industry
	CSEPP Meeting	Alerting Authorities Federal Governance
March 2011	Michigan Association of Broadcaster's Conference	Private Sector Industry
	Congressional Briefings	Federal Governance
	Joint Special Interest Group Emergency Management Practitioners webinar	Alerting Authorities
	NASBA EAS-CAP Webinar	Private Sector Industry
	National Emergency Management Association (NEMA) Mid-Year Meeting	Alerting Authorities
	Tsunami and EAS Demonstration in Virgin Islands	Alerting Authorities Private Sector Industry American People
	Joint Special Interest Group Disseminators webinar	Private Sector Industry
	CTIA Wireless Convention	Private Sector Industry
April 2011	National Association of Broadcasters (NAB) Annual Show 2011	Private Sector Industry
	IPAWS Quarterly Conference calls to RECCWG	Alerting Authorities
	Joint Special Interest Group Emergency Management Practitioners webinar	Alerting Authorities

Month/Year	Event/Activity	Partner Group
April 2011 (cont.)	New Hampshire Emergency Dispatchers Conference	Alerting Authorities
	National Hurricane Conference	Alerting Authorities
	Annual 4 State Gathering	Alerting Authorities
	Joint Special Interest Group Disseminators webinar	Private Sector Industry
	SBE New York Chapter	Private Sector Industry
May 2011	Helping the Hearing Impaired Meeting	Non-Profit and Advocacy
	Twenty First Century Communications Meeting	Private Sector Industry
	Governor's Hurricane Conference	Alerting Authorities Federal Governance
	DHS One Day on the Hill	Federal Governance
	Joint Special Interest Group Emergency Management Practitioners webinar	Alerting Authorities
	Joint Special Interest Group Disseminators webinar	Private Sector Industry
June 2011	NDRN Annual Conference	Non-Profit and Advocacy
	Congressional Briefings	Federal Governance
	DOD JPM Guardian/DHS CBP Workshop	Federal Governance
	NENA (National Emergency Number Association) Conference	Alerting Authorities Private Sector Industry
	New Jersey Broadcasters Association conference	Private Sector Industry
	CSEPP National Workshop	Private Sector Industry
	AMS Weather Warnings and Communications Conference	Alerting Authorities
	Joint Special Interest Group Emergency Management Practitioner webinar	Alerting Authorities
	CWID IPAWS OPEN 2.0 Demonstration	Federal Governance
	RECCWG Region V Meeting	Alerting Authorities
	NWS Summer Partners Meeting	Alerting Authorities Federal Governance
	National UASI and Homeland Security Conference	Alerting Authorities Non-Profit and Advocacy
	Joint Special Interest Group Developers webinar	Private Sector Industry
	EMI Alerting Authorities Focus Group	Alerting Authorities
	EAS Roundtable	Private Sector Industry
July 2011	Americans with Access and Special Functional Needs-IPAWS/ODIC Roundtable	Non-Profit and Advocacy
	IPAWS Quarterly Conference calls to RECCWG	Alerting Authorities
	Puerto Rico Association of Broadcasters Meeting	Private Sector Industry Alerting Authorities
	National Council for Independent Living Annual Conference	Non-Profit and Advocacy
	Joint Special Interest Group Emergency Management Practitioner	Alerting Authorities
	Joint Special Interest Group Developers webinar	Private Sector Industry
August 2011	Tennessee Association of Broadcasters Meeting	Private Sector Industry Alerting Authorities
	Joint Special Interest Group Emergency Management Practitioner webinar	Alerting Authorities
	Texas Association of Broadcasters Meeting	Private Sector Industry Alerting Authorities
	National Information Exchange Model (NIEM) Meeting	Private Sector Industry
	Joint Special Interest Group Developers webinar	Private Sector Industry

Month/Year	Event/Activity	Partner Group
August 2011 (cont.)	Technologies for Critical Incident Preparedness Conference	Private Sector Industry
September 2011	Radio Show	Private Sector Industry
	Joint Special Interest Group Emergency Management Practitioner webinar	Alerting Authorities
	Congressional Briefings	Federal Governance
	Joint Special Interest Group Developers webinar	Private Sector Industry
October 2011	NEMA 2011 Annual Conference	Alerting Authorities
	IPAWS Quarterly Conference calls to RECCWG	Alerting Authorities
	Joint Special Interest Group Emergency Management Practitioner webinar	Alerting Authorities
	Commercial Mobile Alert System (CMAS/PLAN) Test (late 2011)	American People Private Sector Industry Federal Governance Alerting Authorities Non-Profit and Advocacy
	Joint Special Interest Group Developers webinar	Private Sector Industry
	SBE Broadcast & Technology Expo	Private Sector Industry
November 2011	IAEM 2011 Annual Conference	Alerting Authorities Private Sector Industry
	Joint Special Interest Group Emergency Management Practitioner webinar	Alerting Authorities
	SCTE Cable Tech Expo	Private Sector Industry
	Joint Special Interest Group Developers webinar	Private Sector Industry
	National EAS Test (late 2011)	American People Private Sector Industry Federal Governance Alerting Authorities Non-Profit and Advocacy
	National League of Cities	Non-Profit and Advocacy
December 2011	Joint Special Interest Group Emergency Management Practitioner webinar	Alerting Authorities
	Congressional Briefings	Federal Governance
	Joint Special Interest Group Developers webinar	Private Sector Industry
January 2012	Americans with Access and Special Functional Needs-IPAWS/ODIC Roundtable	Non-Profit and Advocacy
	Joint Special Interest Group Emergency Management Practitioner webinar	Alerting Authorities
	Joint Special Interest Group Developers webinar	Private Sector Industry
	IPAWS Quarterly Conference calls to RECCWG	Alerting Authorities
	Consumer Electronic Trade Show	Private Sector Industry
February 2012	Joint Special Interest Group Developers webinar	Private Sector Industry
	NAB/NASBA EAS Town Hall	Private Sector Industry
	CSEPP Meeting	Alerting Authorities Federal Governance
	Joint Special Interest Group Emergency Management Practitioner webinar	Alerting Authorities
March 2012	CTIA—The Wireless Association Annual Conference	Private Sector Industry
	Joint Special Interest Group Emergency Management Practitioner webinar	Alerting Authorities
	National Hurricane Conference	Alerting Authorities

Month/Year	Event/Activity	Partner Group
March 2012 (cont.)	Joint Special Interest Group Developers webinar	Private Sector Industry
	Congressional Briefings	Federal Governance
	National Emergency Management Association (NEMA) Mid-Year Meeting	Alerting Authorities
April 2012	National Association of Broadcasters (NAB) Annual Show 2012	Private Sector Industry
	IPAWS Quarterly Conference calls to RECCWG	Alerting Authorities
	Joint Special Interest Group Emergency Management Practitioner webinar	Alerting Authorities
	Joint Special Interest Group Developers webinar	Private Sector Industry
	IPAWS Quarterly Conference calls to RECCWG	Alerting Authorities
May 2012	Governor's Hurricane Conference	Alerting Authorities Federal Governance
	Joint Special Interest Group Emergency Management Practitioner webinar	Alerting Authorities
	DHS One Day on the Hill	Federal Governance
	Joint Special Interest Group Developers webinar	Private Sector Industry

IPAWS
Integrated Public Alert and Warning System
www.fema.gov/emergency/ipaws